About the Author

Eleanor is thirty and lives in Surrey. With a degree in Film & Popular Culture, she has been writing as a part-time journalist since graduating university, before moving on to poetry in the last year. When she's not writing, she works in a secondary school and has a background in youth work. This is her first poetry collection.

Little Lost Intimacies

Eleanor Jones

Little Lost Intimacies

Olympia Publishers
London

www.olympiapublishers.com
OLYMPIA PAPERBACK EDITION

Copyright © Eleanor Jones 2022

The right of Eleanor Jones to be identified as author of
this work has been asserted in accordance with sections 77 and 78 of
the Copyright, Designs and Patents Act 1988.

All Rights Reserved

No reproduction, copy or transmission of this publication
may be made without written permission.
No paragraph of this publication may be reproduced,
copied or transmitted save with the written permission of the publisher,
or in accordance with the provisions
of the Copyright Act 1956 (as amended).

Any person who commits any unauthorised act in relation to
this publication may be liable to criminal
prosecution and civil claims for damage.

A CIP catalogue record for this title is
available from the British Library.

ISBN: 978-1-80074-805-7

This is a work of fiction.
Names, characters, places and incidents originate from the writer's
imagination. Any resemblance to actual persons, living or dead, is
purely coincidental.

First Published in 2022

Olympia Publishers
Tallis House
2 Tallis Street
London
EC4Y 0AB

Printed in Great Britain

Dedication

For my parents. Who have never made me feel anything less than essential.

Acknowledgements

I am so grateful to Olympia Publishers for bringing my book to life and turning a dream into a reality. I have been collecting poems in my mind for years and I am incredibly thankful to be able to finally see them on paper. Thank you to my parents, Lorraine and Andy, for constantly pushing me to achieve more than I believe myself capable of and for accepting all my quirks and strange interests with humour and love. I would like to thank the small army of women who are my biggest champions and the loves of my life. Thank you to Cara, Jordan, Lucy, Jess, Jenny, Liana, Sophie and Amy. I am so lucky to have you. Thank you to Armin for still being my family after all this time, and for your doubtless faith in my ability to string a sentence together. An enormous thank you to everyone who has ever taken the time to read one of my poems on Instagram and specifically Georgie, who was the first person to read *Little Lost Intimacies*, and whose feedback and encouragement gave me the push I desperately needed. Lastly, a little thank you to Rhys, whose insufferable and wonderful charm has helped remind me a little bit about romance, exactly when I needed it.

HUNGRY

A hunger wholly carnal and cruel in nature, wouldst thou trust in thine fierce appetite?

Righteous tongues roam over rolling hills of heavenly flesh and fevered hands in kind,

Such depths of adoration, under waves of impassioned prayer you will feast at will

Against a flame so wickedly close, shadows dance in spoils of splendour

Limbs remain locked in locomotion, calling for their fill of flavour and formation.

DANCE

Synchronicity in sensuality, bodies bound by the nights strange brooding

The pulse of purple and moody blues, you howl sweetly at this entwinement

No midsummer dream nor spring folly could compare to twilight's tryst

While wicked winds do writhe in tandem, lay boldly beneath this altar of mine.

KINDRED

Wouldst thou kiss these lips of cherry sour? Under the blossom that comes with spring

Adorned with love's own rosy glow, such folly is this meeting of two souls in kind

To dip one's feet into your pools of nectar, hearts will surely tear in tragic fashion

For lips like those which come with poison, gift the longest sleep thine heart divine.

QUAKE

With hearts on sleeves and hopes on edge, lay waste to thoughts of fearful descent

Crawling kisses and limbs soft with lust, weathered souls on the warmest eves

Find me beneath the night's crescent moon, where humble love doth wait in patience

What rapture might this movement bring? One's heart quakes at the thought

Thine bold beating drum is proof still that while the broken may remain just so,

Rhythm doth return to those who so keenly seek it.

POISON

Beg thee kiss the poison from my lips, surrender to eternal sleep

Lay in love for thine soul is but within my close and tender reach

O, won't you indulge in this sweet delirium I deliver to thee,

With all this quaking ecstasy onc offers you so freely?

Merely give yourself over to this indulgence and be mine.

POETRY

Speaking Shakespeare against skin that screams out for sensual touch

Tongue wandering rogue across wayward limbs that part with pleasant ease

Such eagerness to please and pale thighs that flex when fingers caress

Moonlit meetings of romance with lustful intentions made clear.

SUGAR

What a lovely little downfall you have become to me, honey poured upon love hungry minds

Sinking into a sweetness that seeks to rot from within, decaying decadence with sickly satisfaction

Luring hearts in with caramel kisses, such divine deception awaits my mind, body, and soul

Pray go easy on this reluctant romantic for I have felt this shudder of pleasure before

I have ached from a body bent in greedy need and consumed by the sensually starved.

TENDER

Kissing collarbones and tracing fine freckles, tender in arms that sink into seduction

Limbs do melt in mellow release, as twin flames writhe in sweet synchronicity

Bodies together with minds even more so, as feverish need reach euphoric peaks

Tender is the soul that seeks to delve deeper into the pleasure of others.

SECRET

How pulses quicken and chests they do heave in heated corners beyond the crowd

Fingertips find loose strands of hair, while lashes bat with a painful pure longing

The taste of tension is ripe with trepidation while bodies catch up with racing minds

Teasing words and tactful glances hold such power over these pretty playthings

Thine want is showing and lust is written in bold mark across one's needy face.

MEMORY

Hot flashes and cheek flushes at memories of rough thumbs between delicate lips

Vulnerable and vivacious in equal measure, can you recall those moments past?

Left breathless and bold hearted by those hazy eves of candlelight and candour

How they must replay and repeat with fine detail in your ever thinking mind

REST

Syllables slip from parted lips as hands roam across soft and supple curves

Breath quickens and skin shivers while shadows dance across the room

These little lost intimacies haunt the waking hours of such hopeful hearts,

Phantom feelings do plague fitful slumber with such cruel intensity and feverish need.

EXPLORE

Mapping out journeys across a body that has bewitched you so,

How it boldly basks beneath your hungry stare and silky prayer of sweet disposition

Those trailing lips and tips of tongues mark skin with the promise of pleasure

Such a taste of temptation cannot be resisted by minds so eagerly seduced.

ECHO

Shoulders bare and begging for warm breath, fingertips skim sweet collar bones

Limbs lock and linger in the echoes of ecstasy, laying listless once fully fed

Such appetite for one another, how else to live but engorged on heavenly flesh and the long-lasting flavour of sensual satisfaction.

TONGUE

Love is never lost in translation when mouths find each other in the dark

Speaking a language for two when entwined in sheets of cotton and communication

Words and phrases replaced by bodies and movement, a dance we've done before

How you tell tales across my skin with such sweet sophistication.

BOUND

Hair wrapped like ribbons around thick fingers, heat from breath against a slender neck

Anchored by forearms both tanned and toned, at the mercy of all your movement

Divine delirium in this moment of intimacy, hopelessly lost within the caress of you

Shadows sway together against the evening glow, with delicious intentions in mind.

BIRD

The dawn's gentle birdsong brings such softness to our awakening

Limbs entwined in comfortable familiarity, natural and needed

Hair static and eyes sleepy, foreheads bump with old affection

All yawns and stretches, a nip on your shoulder and a squeeze to my thigh

Snooze with me a little longer my love, until we are ready to feast again.

SPORT

Fever dreams of flirtation, those lingering looks and seductive smirks

A tennis match of teasing and temptation; the build, the climb and the rolling thunder

Game, set and match. How I anticipate your every move, but how you please me so.

SPREAD

The smell of your skin lingers long after you have left me, cheap sheets and cheaper wine

The memory of thighs spread and secrets escaping from gasping breaths

The clock was ticking beside us while time stood still between us

Now phantom feelings haunt my limbs as they flex in hopeless longing

While my heart aches for the return of you, my body begs even more so.

BURIAL

Kill me with kisses and caresses, under skies so moody and heavy with wanting

Lay down this body for worship with wild, passionate abandonment

To tip into madness by your twisted tongue would be a blessing so,

I bow to an ending of enduring a pleasure so intense and unyielding.

WOLF

Howl with me against the full moon with carnal desire in mind

Savaged hearts and bodies broken mend together while curled and buried within each other

Souls spent in new pleasures of the flesh and feelings renewed

Breathing fresh air into my lungs and flames between my thighs

Throw caution to the wind and strip your soul of sadness underneath the sheets.

WORSHIP

My tongue still holds the taste of you, while you snooze beneath the sheets

The scent of our undoing still lingers in the air, stirring my senses once more

A map of stars across your skin in flecks of colour that glow in the early hours

To watch you lay in such soft slumber stirs a quiet love within me

A gentle flame within my darkest chambers, one sparked by your kindness and stoked by your passion for my pleasure.

RENAISSANCE

Staring down at me underneath that silver glow, our skin glistening with the moon's magic kiss

Have two souls ever been so better suited in sensuality?

O, how you worship this vessel I have long wept over in quiet embarrassment and despair

Yet here I am, basking in the glory of me and mine with your hands performing such healing

You whisper scripture against every fold and curve of my divine flesh

Your wanting fuels my own, what a gift you have given.

FULL

When eyes locked and limbs entwined, a silent agreement was made

To treat each other's souls with tender trepidation, not to greedily consume each other's energy

For despite the feast of fevered flesh, it is thine soul that leaves me so satisfied

Lay with me in trust and hope, let us drink from one another

Small sips to keep us quenched, my love.

MUSIC

Your gentle breath in the dark is a symphony of adoration

What delight explodes in my heart at the knowledge that you are there

In deep slumber though you are, your presence is bold and beautiful

How sweet it is to lay with you, in the aftermath of our binding

Sweet sweat and scars of desperate need, let me linger in this moment of solitude.

LITERATURE

I can recall the way the window was cracked just so, how the chill felt on my pale bare skin

The way our heart rates finally slowed and steadied with that spark in the air of something new

If the memory were pages, I would have read them to tatters, my favourite chapter from my favourite book

Write sequels with me and let us relive this fine moment.

SECRET

The rolling mist that brings the dawn breathes new life into my tired lungs

I trace constellations across your skin, stealing secret moments before you stir

These early morning intimacies we share without your even knowing

Let me love you from afar while remaining close enough to soak you in.

MEMORY

I know that you remember how it felt to taste that ecstasy

When you made up for all your failings in those hazy afternoons

With minds caught on fire and limbs locked together, say you remember how it felt to call my name

You would succumb to my calling with such little fight, yet here you are pretending that you can resist me once again.

GLOW

Your cherry lips found mine as if it were their one and only purpose,

I recall the way I melted into your waiting embrace

How natural it all had felt, as if bewitched by something wonderful

Delightfully intoxicated by the light shining from your face.

STICKY

He called her peaches in the afternoons, for that is when she was her sweetest

With lips that spilled lyrical nonsense she would cast spells of dizzying mischief

For hours they lay bewitched by one another, sipping on golden nectar

Peaches until the morning light, he was transfixed by such summer treats.

CURVE

If self-loathing be the thief of love, then thy lips of restoration have spilled reminders of what beauty one beholds

Planting seeds of delight and delirious joy, soon it blooms across the divine self and the curved softness given in gift

So spellbound is thines hungry heart, salacious need and sweet offerings blend together to create this elixir we name love and loving.

Printed in Great Britain
by Amazon